ASOGWA JOY LOVE

Endurance Within

Copyright © 2024 by Asogwa Joy Love

All rights reserved. No part of this publication may be reproduced, stored or transmitted in any form or by any means, electronic, mechanical, photocopying, recording, scanning, or otherwise without written permission from the publisher. It is illegal to copy this book, post it to a website, or distribute it by any other means without permission.

Asogwa Joy Love asserts the moral right to be identified as the author of this work.

Asogwa Joy Love has no responsibility for the persistence or accuracy of URLs for external or third-party Internet Websites referred to in this publication and does not guarantee that any content on such Websites is, or will remain, accurate or appropriate.

First edition

This book was professionally typeset on Reedsy.
Find out more at reedsy.com

Contents

1	The Inciting Incident	1
2	Unraveling the Mystery	5
3	The First Confrontation	10
4	Allies and Enemies	15
5	Shadows in the Dark	20
6	The Final Countdown	25
7	Infiltration	30
8	Into the Lion's Den	35
9	The Hidden Betrayal	39
10	The Trap	44
11	The Double Cross	48
12	The Final Gambit	53

1

The Inciting Incident

The sun dipped below the horizon, casting long shadows across the quiet suburban street where Alex Parker lived. The house at 34 Elmwood Drive stood serene, its windows glowing with the soft light of the evening. Inside, Alex sat at his kitchen table, finishing his dinner while his wife, Emily, put their young daughter, Lily, to bed. The ordinary tranquility of the scene was deceptive, hiding the storm about to break over their lives.

Alex's thoughts drifted to the promotion he was expecting at work. It had been a long time coming, and he had worked tirelessly for it. He was lost in a daydream about the future when the doorbell rang, its sharp tone cutting through the stillness of the night. Alex glanced at the clock on the wall. It was unusual for anyone to visit at this hour.

He pushed his chair back, walked to the door, and opened it. There was no one there. Alex stepped onto the porch, scanning the darkened street, but it was empty. As he turned to go back inside, he noticed a plain white envelope lying on the welcome mat. Frowning, he picked it up and examined it under the porch light. There was no name or address, just his family's initials scrawled on the front: "A, E, L."

Puzzled, Alex tore open the envelope and unfolded the single sheet of paper inside. The message was short and chilling: "You have something we want. If you don't comply, your family will pay the price."

Alex's heart pounded in his chest as he read and reread the words. What could they possibly mean? He had no enemies, no debts, nothing that could provoke such a threat. He walked back inside, the letter clutched in his hand, and locked the door behind him. Emily was coming down the stairs, a tired smile on her face.

"Who was it?" she asked.

Alex hesitated, considering whether to tell her about the letter. But the look of worry on his face betrayed him, and Emily's smile faded.

"What's wrong?"

He handed her the letter without a word. As she read it, her face paled, and she looked up at him with wide, fearful eyes.

"Alex, what is this? Who would send something like this?"

"I don't know," he replied, his mind racing. "But I need to find out."

They sat at the kitchen table, the letter between them, discussing what to do. Calling the police seemed like the obvious choice, but Alex feared it might escalate the situation. He decided to investigate further before involving the authorities. He needed to understand the threat, and he needed to do it quickly.

The next morning, Alex left for work earlier than usual, the letter tucked safely in his briefcase. He spent the day distracted, barely able to focus on his tasks. At lunch, he called in a favor from a friend who worked in private security. They met in a small café, where Alex explained the situation and handed over the letter.

His friend, Mark, examined the letter carefully. "This isn't a prank, Alex. Whoever wrote this means business. We need to find out what they want and why they're targeting you."

"That's what I was hoping you could help with," Alex said, his voice tight with worry.

"I'll run this through our databases, see if we can trace the paper, the ink, anything that might give us a lead," Mark replied. "In the meantime, keep your eyes open. Don't do anything out of the ordinary, and make sure Emily and Lily are safe."

Alex nodded, feeling a bit of relief knowing that Mark was on the case. He returned to work, trying to focus on his tasks but finding it nearly impossible. The minutes dragged by, each one filled with a sense of impending doom.

That evening, Alex returned home to find Emily on the phone with her mother, trying to act normal but failing miserably. Lily was playing with her dolls in the living room, blissfully unaware of the tension that gripped her parents.

After dinner, as Alex sat in his study, his phone buzzed with a message from Mark. It was a single line: "We need to meet. Urgent."

Alex's pulse quickened. He grabbed his keys and told Emily he had to run an errand. She looked worried but didn't press him. He drove to the address Mark had sent, a secluded parking lot on the outskirts of town.

Mark was waiting in his car, the engine running. Alex got in, and Mark handed him a folder.

"We found something," Mark said, his tone grim. "The paper is custom-made, used by a very specific group. These people are serious, Alex. They don't make threats lightly."

Alex opened the folder and scanned the contents. His blood ran cold as he realized the magnitude of the situation. The group in question had a reputation for ruthless efficiency and a history of making their threats a reality.

"We need to find out what they want from you," Mark continued. "And we need to do it fast. Until we know more, you and your family are in grave danger."

Alex nodded, his mind racing. The peaceful life he had known was slipping away, replaced by a shadowy world of threats and uncertainty. But one thing was clear: he would do whatever it took to protect his family. The journey ahead would test his resolve, but he was determined to face it head-on. As he drove home, Alex's grip tightened on the steering wheel, his jaw set with determination. The first steps of his perilous journey had begun, and there was no turning back.

2

Unraveling the Mystery

The next morning, Alex awoke with a heavy sense of dread. Emily was still asleep, and the house was eerily quiet. He slipped out of bed, careful not to wake her, and made his way downstairs. As he brewed a pot of coffee, his mind replayed the events of the previous day. The letter, the meeting with Mark, and the disturbing revelations about the group targeting him. He knew he needed answers, and he needed them fast.

After dropping Lily off at school, Alex headed to his office, his thoughts consumed by the mystery. He decided to take a personal day, knowing he wouldn't be able to focus on work. Instead, he drove to Mark's office, hoping his friend had made progress overnight.

Mark greeted him with a grim expression. "I've been digging all night, Alex. This group, they call themselves The Consortium. They're involved in high-stakes blackmail, corporate espionage, and worse. They don't usually target ordinary people, which makes your situation even more perplexing."

Alex felt a chill run down his spine. "Why me? What could they possibly want from me?"

"We need to find out," Mark said. "I have some contacts who might be able to help. But we need to be careful. The Consortium has eyes everywhere."

They spent the next few hours compiling information, cross-referencing names and incidents, trying to piece together any connections. Mark's office was filled with the hum of computers and the rustle of paper as they worked tirelessly.

Around noon, Mark received a call. He stepped outside to take it, leaving Alex alone with his thoughts. Alex's phone buzzed with a new message. It was from an unknown number: "Stop investigating, or there will be consequences."

His heart pounded as he showed the message to Mark when he returned. "They know we're looking into them. We need to be more cautious," Mark said, his face set with determination.

They decided to meet one of Mark's contacts, a former Consortium member who had turned informant. The rendezvous was set for a remote warehouse on the outskirts of the city. As Alex and Mark drove there, the tension in the car was palpable.

The warehouse loomed in the distance, a dilapidated structure that seemed abandoned. They parked a distance away and approached on foot, the gravel crunching under their shoes. Inside, the dim light cast long shadows, and the air was thick with dust.

A figure emerged from the darkness. "You're Alex Parker?" the man asked, his voice low and wary.

Alex nodded. "And you're the informant?"

The man, who introduced himself as Tom, glanced around nervously. "I don't have much time. The Consortium doesn't take kindly to betrayal. But I can tell you this: they want something you have, something valuable. Think hard, Alex. What could you possess that they would go to these lengths for?"

Alex racked his brain. "I'm just an ordinary guy. I work a regular job, have a family. There's nothing special about me."

Tom shook his head. "No one is truly ordinary, Alex. Look at your past, your connections. There must be something."

Suddenly, the sound of footsteps echoed through the warehouse. Tom's eyes widened with fear. "They're here. You need to go. Now!"

Before they could react, figures emerged from the shadows, guns drawn. Mark pulled Alex behind a stack of crates, and they ducked as bullets whizzed past. Tom tried to flee but was caught in the crossfire, collapsing to the ground with a pained cry.

Alex's mind raced as they crouched behind the crates, trying to come up with a plan. Mark motioned for him to stay low and follow his lead. They moved slowly, inching towards an exit at the back of the warehouse.

As they neared the door, one of the gunmen spotted them and shouted. Mark pushed Alex through the door and slammed it shut, jamming a metal rod through the handle to buy them some time.

They ran through the maze of alleyways outside the warehouse, their breath coming in ragged gasps. Behind them, they could hear the gunmen giving chase. They turned a corner and stumbled upon an old, abandoned car. Mark quickly jimmied the lock, and they climbed inside, hoping the gunmen would lose their trail.

For several tense minutes, they sat in silence, listening for any signs of pursuit. When they were sure the coast was clear, Mark started the car and they drove away, putting as much distance between themselves and the warehouse as possible.

"That was too close," Mark said, his knuckles white on the steering wheel. "We need to be more careful. They know we're onto them."

Alex nodded, his mind still reeling from the encounter. "Tom said they want something valuable. I can't think of anything."

"Think about your job, your colleagues, your past. There has to be a connection," Mark urged.

As they drove back to town, Alex's thoughts turned to his work. He was an analyst at a tech firm, handling sensitive data and projects. Could something from his work be the key? He made a mental note to dig deeper into his recent assignments, looking for anything out of the ordinary.

Back at Mark's office, they regrouped and reviewed the information they had gathered. Alex's mind kept returning to a project he had worked on recently, involving advanced encryption technology. It was cutting-edge and highly confidential. Could The Consortium be after this?

"Mark, there's a project at work, something new. Advanced encryption. It's top secret, and I've been working on it closely. Could that be what they're after?"

Mark considered it. "It's possible. If this technology is as valuable as it sounds, it could be worth a lot to the right people. We need to find out who else knows about this project and if there have been any breaches in security."

As night fell, Alex returned home, his mind racing with new leads and unanswered questions. He hugged Emily and Lily tightly, feeling the weight of the threat hanging over them. He knew he couldn't stop now. The safety of his family depended on unraveling this mystery.

He spent the evening going through his work documents, looking for any signs of unusual activity. His determination grew with each passing hour, fueled by the need to protect his loved ones. The road ahead was fraught with danger, but Alex was resolved to see it through. He would uncover the truth, no matter the cost.

3

The First Confrontation

Alex sat in his dimly lit study, the glow of his computer screen casting eerie shadows across the room. He had spent the better part of the night digging through his work files, searching for any anomalies related to the encryption project. The Consortium's intentions were still a mystery, but he was determined to uncover the truth. The weight of the situation pressed heavily on his shoulders, and the thought of Emily and Lily's safety kept him focused.

As dawn broke, Alex's eyes burned from lack of sleep. He was about to shut down his computer when a file caught his attention. It was a recent email from a colleague named David Larson, marked with high priority. The email detailed an unexpected system breach that had been swiftly contained. Alex's pulse quickened. This could be the lead he needed.

He quickly dressed and headed to the office, arriving before most of his colleagues. The building was eerily quiet, amplifying his anxiety. He made his way to David's office, knocking lightly on the door. David looked up from his desk, surprise evident on his face.

THE FIRST CONFRONTATION

"Alex, what are you doing here so early?" David asked, setting down his coffee.

"I need to talk to you about the system breach," Alex said, closing the door behind him. "Why didn't you mention it to me earlier?"

David's expression turned wary. "It was contained quickly, and we didn't want to cause unnecessary alarm. Why are you so interested?"

"There's more at stake here than you realize," Alex replied, his voice low. "I've received threats. My family is in danger, and I believe it's connected to our work."

David's eyes widened. "Threats? Are you sure?"

Alex nodded, pulling out the ominous letter from his briefcase and handing it to David. "They're targeting me because of something I have. I think it's related to the encryption project."

David read the letter, his face growing paler with each word. "This is serious. We need to get ahead of this. Let's check the security logs again, see if we missed anything."

Together, they delved into the system's security logs, poring over lines of code and timestamps. Hours passed with no breakthroughs, and Alex's frustration mounted. Just as he was about to give up, David pointed to an entry that seemed out of place. It was a data transfer marked with a foreign IP address, occurring around the time of the breach.

"This shouldn't be here," David said, frowning. "This IP address doesn't belong to any of our partners or clients."

Alex's heart raced. "Can you trace it?"

David nodded, typing furiously on his keyboard. "Give me a few minutes."

As David worked, Alex's phone buzzed with a call from Mark. He stepped out into the hallway to answer.

"Alex, I've been digging too. The Consortium has been unusually active lately, targeting tech firms and government contracts. They're after something big."

"I think we found a lead," Alex said, glancing back at David. "There was a data transfer during the breach. We're tracing it now."

"Be careful," Mark warned. "These people are dangerous. Keep me updated."

Alex returned to David's office just as the screen flashed with new information. "Got it," David said. "The IP address is registered to a shell company. It's a front for The Consortium."

Alex's blood ran cold. "That's it. We need to act fast."

David agreed to help, and they compiled all the information they had on the breach and the encryption project. As they prepared to leave, the office intercom crackled to life.

"Alex Parker, please report to the front desk. You have a visitor."

Alex and David exchanged a wary glance. "I wasn't expecting anyone," Alex said, his heart pounding.

"Be careful," David urged. "It could be them."

Alex made his way to the front desk, every step filled with trepidation. A man in a dark suit stood waiting, his expression unreadable. "Mr. Parker," the man said, extending a hand. "I'm Agent Thomas with the FBI. We need to talk."

THE FIRST CONFRONTATION

Alex felt a mix of relief and suspicion. "FBI? How did you know to come here?"

"We've been monitoring The Consortium for some time," Agent Thomas replied. "We intercepted communications indicating they were targeting you. We need your cooperation to bring them down."

Alex hesitated, his mind racing. Could he trust this agent? He glanced around, noticing the wary looks from his colleagues. "What do you need from me?"

"Let's talk somewhere private," Agent Thomas suggested, gesturing towards a conference room.

They entered the room, and Agent Thomas closed the door behind them. "We believe The Consortium is planning a major operation involving the encryption technology you've been working on. We need your help to stop them."

Alex nodded slowly. "I want to protect my family. I'll do whatever it takes."

Agent Thomas handed Alex a secure phone. "Use this to contact me directly. We'll be in touch with further instructions. And Alex, be vigilant. They won't hesitate to act if they feel threatened."

As the agent left, Alex felt a renewed sense of urgency. He returned to David's office, where his friend was waiting anxiously.

"What happened?" David asked.

"FBI. They're monitoring The Consortium. We need to be careful," Alex replied, his mind already racing with plans.

They spent the rest of the day securing their work and preparing for the next steps. As evening approached, Alex gathered his things and headed home, feeling the weight of the day's revelations. He knew the road ahead would be fraught with danger, but his determination had only grown stronger.

That night, as Alex lay in bed, he felt Emily stir beside him. She turned to face him, her eyes filled with concern. "Are you okay?"

"I will be," Alex said, wrapping his arms around her. "I promise I'll keep us safe."

Outside, the night was still, but Alex knew the storm was far from over. The first confrontation had only just begun, and he was ready to face whatever came next.

4

Allies and Enemies

The next few days passed in a blur of activity and anxiety. Alex's every waking moment was consumed by the threat hanging over his family. The house, usually a haven of comfort, felt like a fortress under siege. He had taken Agent Thomas's advice to heart, installing additional security measures and keeping a close watch on any unusual activity around their home.

Emily sensed the heightened tension but respected Alex's need for secrecy. Their once open and light-hearted conversations were now replaced by quiet, loaded glances and brief exchanges of necessary information. It was clear to both of them that their lives had irrevocably changed.

Alex's phone buzzed, breaking the uneasy silence of the evening. It was Mark. "I've got a lead. Meet me at the coffee shop on Fifth. And Alex, be careful."

Alex nodded, though Mark couldn't see him. "I will."

He told Emily he had to run an errand and promised he'd be back soon. The drive to the coffee shop was tense, his mind racing with possibilities. He arrived to find Mark already seated in a corner, a stack of papers and a laptop in front of him.

"Thanks for coming," Mark said, motioning for Alex to sit. "I've been digging into that shell company connected to the IP address. It's more than just a front. It's part of a network used by The Consortium for illicit activities. Money laundering, illegal data trading, you name it."

Alex leaned forward, his pulse quickening. "What do we do next?"

"I've arranged a meeting with someone who might help us," Mark said. "An insider. She's willing to talk, but we need to be discreet. Her life is at risk, just like yours."

"Where and when?"

"Tonight. 9 PM. An old warehouse by the docks. She insisted on a neutral location."

Alex nodded, feeling a mix of anticipation and dread. "I'll be there."

The hours dragged by as Alex waited for the meeting time. He went through the motions of dinner and bedtime with Emily and Lily, his mind elsewhere. When the time came, he kissed Emily goodbye and told her to lock the doors behind him. She looked worried but didn't ask questions.

The drive to the docks was filled with tension. The area was deserted, the only sound the distant lapping of waves against the pier. Alex parked his car and made his way to the designated warehouse. Mark was waiting outside, his face grim in the dim light.

"She's inside," Mark said, nodding towards the door. "Let's go."

The interior of the warehouse was dark and musty, the air thick with the scent of saltwater and rust. A single light bulb flickered above a makeshift table, casting long shadows. A woman stood by the table, her posture tense. She had dark hair pulled back into a ponytail and sharp eyes that darted around the room, assessing every shadow.

"This is Alex," Mark said by way of introduction. "Alex, this is Maria. She used to work for The Consortium."

Maria nodded curtly. "I don't have much time. They'll notice I'm gone soon."

"What can you tell us?" Alex asked, his voice barely above a whisper.

"The Consortium is after your encryption project," Maria said, her tone urgent. "They plan to use it to break into secure government and corporate systems. They've already made significant progress, thanks to the data they've stolen from your company."

Alex felt a cold wave of fear wash over him. "Why me? Why target me specifically?"

Maria hesitated, then reached into her bag and pulled out a file. "Because you're the key. You designed the encryption algorithm they need. Without your knowledge, they can't complete their plans."

Alex took the file, his hands trembling. "How do we stop them?"

"We need to expose them," Maria said. "Gather evidence, bring it to the authorities. But we have to be careful. They have eyes and ears everywhere."

As they spoke, the sound of footsteps echoed through the warehouse. Maria's eyes widened with fear. "They're here."

Mark drew his gun, motioning for Alex to stay behind him. The door burst open, and a group of armed men stormed in, their faces hidden behind masks. Maria darted towards the shadows, trying to escape, but a gunshot rang out, and she fell to the ground with a scream.

Alex's heart pounded in his chest as he and Mark took cover behind a stack of crates. The air was filled with the deafening roar of gunfire. Mark returned fire, but they were outnumbered and outgunned.

"We need to get out of here!" Mark shouted over the noise.

Alex nodded, his mind racing. He grabbed the file Maria had given him and shoved it into his jacket. They made their way towards a side exit, bullets whizzing past them. As they burst through the door, they found themselves in a narrow alley, their path blocked by another group of armed men.

Mark fired off a few rounds, buying them a momentary respite. "Go! I'll cover you!"

"I'm not leaving you!" Alex shouted, but Mark shoved him forward.

"Go! Now!"

With no other choice, Alex ran. He could hear the sounds of the struggle behind him, Mark's shouts and the gunmen's curses. He didn't stop running until he reached his car. He fumbled with the keys, his hands shaking, and finally managed to start the engine.

He sped away from the docks, his heart racing, his mind a blur of fear and adrenaline. He had the file, but at what cost? He prayed that Mark would be okay, but deep down, he knew the situation was dire.

When he finally reached the safety of his home, he collapsed onto the couch, gasping for breath. Emily rushed to his side, her face pale with worry.

"What happened?" she asked, her voice trembling.

Alex held her close, his mind still reeling from the night's events. "We're in deeper than I thought," he said, his voice raw with emotion. "But we have a chance. We have the evidence. We just need to stay one step ahead."

As the reality of their situation sank in, Alex knew that their fight was far from over. The lines between allies and enemies were blurred, and danger lurked around every corner. But he was determined to see this through, to protect his family and bring The Consortium to justice. The road ahead was uncertain, but Alex's resolve was stronger than ever.

5

Shadows in the Dark

The following morning, Alex woke with a start, the events of the previous night replaying in his mind. Mark's fate was unknown, and Maria's death weighed heavily on him. He knew he had to act quickly, but he felt a deep sense of helplessness. The file he had taken from Maria lay on the coffee table, its presence a grim reminder of the stakes.

Emily sat across from him, worry etched on her face. "Alex, you have to tell me what's going on. I can't help if I don't know."

Alex hesitated. He had tried to protect her from the danger, but he realized now that she was already deeply involved. He reached for her hand and began to explain everything – the letter, The Consortium, the encryption project, and the meeting with Maria.

Emily listened intently, her eyes widening with each revelation. "This is serious. We need to get help."

"I know," Alex said. "I'm meeting with Agent Thomas today. He said he'd have more information for us."

The drive to the FBI office was tense. Alex kept glancing at the rearview mirror, half-expecting to see a tail. The city felt different now, every stranger a potential threat, every shadow a hiding place for enemies. When they arrived, Agent Thomas was waiting for them, his expression grave.

"Come with me," he said, leading them to a secure conference room. Once inside, he turned to Alex. "We've had some developments. Mark is in the hospital. He was injured, but he's alive."

Relief flooded through Alex. "Thank God. What about The Consortium? Do we have enough to go after them?"

"We're building our case," Agent Thomas replied. "But we need more concrete evidence. What did you get from Maria?"

Alex handed over the file. "She said this would help. It's everything she had on The Consortium's operations."

Agent Thomas flipped through the pages, his expression growing more serious. "This is good. It's a start. But we'll need to corroborate this with more intel. We've got a lead on one of their safe houses. We're planning a raid tonight."

"I want to help," Alex said, surprising himself with the firmness of his words.

Agent Thomas shook his head. "It's too dangerous. Let us handle it. Your priority should be keeping your family safe."

Before Alex could argue, the door opened, and another agent stepped in. "Sir, we've got a situation. We just intercepted a communication. The Consortium knows about the raid. They're planning an ambush."

Agent Thomas swore under his breath. "We need to move now. Alex, I want you and your family to stay here. You'll be safe in our protective custody."

Alex's mind raced. He hated the idea of sitting idly by, but he knew Agent Thomas was right. He nodded reluctantly. "Okay. Just promise me you'll bring these people down."

Thomas's expression softened. "We will. Stay safe, Alex."

As the agents mobilized for the raid, Alex and Emily were escorted to a secure room. The hours dragged by in excruciating silence. Alex paced the small space, his thoughts a whirlwind of fear and anticipation. Emily sat on the edge of the bed, trying to keep a brave face for Lily, who had fallen asleep in her lap.

Finally, the door opened, and Agent Thomas stepped in, looking weary but determined. "The raid was successful. We apprehended several key members of The Consortium. But their leader, Victor Crane, escaped. We're tracking him now."

"Crane," Alex repeated, the name sending a shiver down his spine. "He's the one behind all this?"

"Yes," Thomas said. "And he's dangerous. We'll do everything we can to bring him in, but you need to be vigilant."

The days that followed were a blur of heightened security measures and constant updates from the FBI. Alex and his family were moved to a safe house, their location kept secret even from their closest friends. Alex tried to maintain a semblance of normalcy for Emily and Lily, but the fear and tension were palpable.

One night, as Alex was going through the file Maria had given him, he noticed a small, hidden pocket inside the folder. He carefully opened it and found a USB drive. His heart skipped a beat. This could be the key to everything.

He plugged the drive into his laptop, his hands trembling. The screen lit up with a series of encrypted files. He worked quickly, using his expertise to decrypt the data. What he found made his blood run cold. Detailed plans of The Consortium's operations, names of high-profile targets, and blueprints for a cyberattack that could cripple major infrastructures.

"This is it," he whispered. "This is the proof we need."

He called Agent Thomas immediately, explaining what he had found. "We need to act fast. This information could be their downfall."

Thomas agreed. "I'm sending a team to secure the drive. Stay put until they arrive."

Alex's heart pounded as he waited. Every sound outside the safe house seemed magnified, every shadow a potential threat. When the team arrived, he handed over the drive, feeling a mixture of relief and anxiety.

"You've done well, Alex," Thomas said. "This could be the breakthrough we've been waiting for."

But as the agents left, Alex couldn't shake the feeling that they were still in danger. The Consortium was ruthless, and they wouldn't go down without a fight. He looked at Emily and Lily, who were watching him with wide, worried eyes.

The night passed slowly, every creak and whisper keeping Alex on edge. He barely slept, his mind racing with plans and contingencies. Just before dawn, his phone buzzed with a message from Agent Thomas: "We've traced Crane's location. It's time to end this."

Alex knew what he had to do. He couldn't stay on the sidelines any longer. He kissed Emily and Lily, promising he'd return soon. As he left the safe house, a steely determination settled over him. He was ready to face Victor Crane and bring an end to The Consortium's reign of terror.

6

The Final Countdown

The night air was thick with anticipation as Alex drove towards the location Agent Thomas had provided. Every mile brought him closer to the showdown that could determine the fate of his family and countless others. The address led him to an abandoned factory on the outskirts of town, its silhouette looming against the moonlit sky like a forgotten giant.

Alex parked a few blocks away and made his way to the rendezvous point, a small clearing hidden by dense trees. The FBI team was already there, crouched in the shadows, their faces grim and determined. Agent Thomas approached Alex, handing him a bulletproof vest and a comms device.

"We've got one shot at this," Thomas said, his voice a low whisper. "Crane is inside, but he's heavily guarded. Our intel suggests he's planning to launch the cyberattack tonight. We need to stop him before he can execute his plan."

Alex nodded, strapping on the vest. "I'm ready."

Thomas gestured to the team, and they moved silently towards the factory, their footsteps muffled by the soft ground. As they neared the entrance,

Thomas signaled for them to split into two groups. Alex followed Thomas, his heart pounding in his chest.

The factory's entrance was guarded by two men. Thomas took them out swiftly, a flurry of precise movements leaving them unconscious on the ground. They slipped inside, the interior a maze of dark corridors and rusted machinery. The air smelled of oil and decay, the silence broken only by the faint hum of machinery deep within the building.

They moved cautiously, scanning each corner for threats. The team communicated through hand signals, their movements synchronized and efficient. As they neared the heart of the factory, the hum grew louder, accompanied by the sound of typing and low voices.

Thomas held up a hand, signaling for them to stop. He pointed towards a doorway at the end of the hall. Alex could see a faint light spilling out, casting long shadows on the floor. They crept closer, peering through the doorway.

Inside was a makeshift control room, filled with computers and monitors displaying streams of data. At the center stood Victor Crane, his back to the door, flanked by armed guards. He was barking orders, his voice cold and commanding.

"Prepare for the final sequence," Crane said. "Once the attack is initiated, there's no turning back."

Thomas nodded to the team, and they burst into the room, weapons drawn. "FBI! Drop your weapons!"

Chaos erupted. The guards opened fire, and the room was filled with the deafening roar of gunshots. Alex ducked behind a console, his heart racing. He returned fire, taking down one of the guards. The team moved with practiced precision, quickly gaining the upper hand.

Crane turned, his eyes narrowing as he spotted Alex. "You," he hissed, reaching for a gun. Before he could fire, Alex tackled him, the two men crashing to the ground. They grappled for control, the room spinning around them in a blur of motion.

Crane was stronger than he looked, his grip like iron. But Alex fought with a determination born of desperation. He thought of Emily and Lily, of the lives at stake, and a surge of strength coursed through him. He managed to knock the gun from Crane's hand, sending it skidding across the floor.

"You're too late," Crane snarled, his eyes wild with fury. "The countdown has started. You can't stop it now."

Alex glanced at the monitors, seeing the countdown timer ticking down with relentless precision. 00:05... 00:04... 00:03...

"Thomas!" Alex shouted. "We need to stop the countdown!"

Thomas rushed to the console, his fingers flying over the keyboard. "I'm trying, but the system's locked down. We need the override code."

Crane laughed, a harsh, grating sound. "You'll never get it from me."

Alex's mind raced. He remembered the USB drive Maria had given him, the encrypted files detailing The Consortium's operations. There had to be something in there. He reached into his pocket, pulling out the drive and handing it to Thomas.

"Try this. There might be something in the files."

Thomas plugged in the drive, scanning the contents. His eyes lit up as he found what he was looking for. "Got it. Hold them off, I need a few more seconds."

Alex turned back to Crane, who was struggling to his feet. He landed a punch, sending Crane sprawling back to the ground. The guards were down, the team securing the room, but the timer continued to count down. 00:02... 00:01...

"Hurry, Thomas!" Alex shouted, his voice raw with urgency.

Thomas typed furiously, the seconds ticking away. Just as the timer hit 00:00, the screen flashed and the countdown froze. The room fell silent, the tension hanging thick in the air. Thomas let out a breath he hadn't realized he was holding.

"It's done," he said, turning to Alex. "We stopped it."

Crane glared at them, his face twisted with rage. "You may have won this battle, but the war is far from over."

Alex felt a surge of triumph mixed with exhaustion. "We'll see about that."

The team secured Crane and the remaining guards, leading them out of the factory. As Alex stepped outside, the first light of dawn was breaking over the horizon. The nightmare was far from over, but they had won a crucial victory. He knew there would be more battles to come, more challenges to face. But for now, he allowed himself a moment of relief.

Agent Thomas approached him, clapping a hand on his shoulder. "You did good, Alex. We couldn't have done this without you."

Alex nodded, feeling a sense of camaraderie and purpose. "What happens now?"

"We'll interrogate Crane, gather more intel, and keep dismantling The Consortium piece by piece. It's going to be a long fight, but we'll see it through."

Alex looked out over the city, the dawn light casting a new perspective on the familiar skyline. He thought of Emily and Lily, waiting for him at the safe house. He had fought to protect them, and he would continue to fight, no matter the cost.

As he walked back to his car, the weight of the night's events settled over him. But there was also a newfound resolve. He had faced the shadows in the dark and emerged stronger. The journey ahead was uncertain, but he was ready to face it, one step at a time.

7

Infiltration

The sun had barely risen when Alex returned to the safe house, his mind still buzzing with the events of the night. Emily met him at the door, her eyes wide with worry. "Are you okay? What happened?"

Alex pulled her into a tight embrace, feeling the tension in his muscles slowly ease. "We stopped the attack. Crane is in custody."

Emily sighed with relief, but her expression remained troubled. "What happens now?"

Alex looked into her eyes, seeing the fear and determination mirrored there. "We keep fighting. We dismantle The Consortium piece by piece until they're no longer a threat."

Emily nodded, understanding the gravity of their situation. "We're in this together, Alex. Whatever it takes."

Later that day, Agent Thomas arrived at the safe house, his face a mask of determination. "Alex, we need to talk. We've gotten some new intel from

Crane's interrogation. It's urgent."

They gathered in the living room, the tension palpable. Thomas laid out a series of blueprints and documents on the coffee table. "We've discovered that The Consortium has another facility, a hidden lab where they're developing advanced hacking tools. It's in the city, heavily guarded and nearly impenetrable."

Alex studied the blueprints, his mind racing. "What's the plan?"

"We need to get inside and gather evidence," Thomas said. "But we can't just storm the place. We need someone on the inside, someone who can disable the security systems and help us gain access."

Alex's heart skipped a beat. "You want me to infiltrate the facility."

Thomas nodded. "You have the skills and the knowledge. And most importantly, they won't be expecting you. We'll support you remotely, but once you're inside, you'll be on your own."

Emily gripped Alex's hand tightly. "Are you sure about this? It's dangerous."

Alex looked at her, seeing the fear in her eyes, but also the unspoken trust. "I have to do this, Emily. It's the only way to keep you and Lily safe."

That night, Alex prepared for the mission, his mind focused and sharp. He equipped himself with the tools he would need – a laptop, hacking devices, and a concealed weapon. Agent Thomas gave him a small earpiece for communication and a device to disable the security systems.

"Remember, we'll be monitoring you the entire time," Thomas said. "If things go south, we'll extract you as quickly as possible."

Alex nodded, feeling the weight of the responsibility on his shoulders. He kissed Emily and Lily goodbye, promising he would return soon. As he left the safe house, he steeled himself for what lay ahead.

The facility was located in an industrial district, surrounded by high fences and patrolled by armed guards. Alex parked a safe distance away and approached the perimeter on foot, keeping to the shadows. He located a small maintenance gate, just as the blueprints had indicated, and used his tools to disable the lock.

Slipping inside, he made his way through the darkened corridors, avoiding the security cameras and patrols. His heart pounded in his chest, every sound magnified in the silence. He reached the central control room, where the main security systems were located.

"Thomas, I'm in position," he whispered into the earpiece.

"Good. Now, disable the security grid. We'll guide you from there."

Alex plugged his device into the control panel, his fingers flying over the keyboard. The system was complex, but he managed to bypass the encryption and shut down the security cameras and alarms. The screens went dark, and he felt a surge of triumph.

"I'm in. What's next?"

"Proceed to the main lab. It's down the hall to your left. Be careful."

Alex moved quickly, the darkness his ally. He reached the lab door and used his tools to unlock it. Inside, the room was filled with high-tech equipment and computers, the air humming with energy. He approached one of the terminals and began downloading the data onto his laptop.

Suddenly, a sound behind him made him freeze. He turned to see a figure standing in the doorway, a gun aimed at his chest.

"Step away from the computer," the man said, his voice cold and commanding.

Alex's mind raced. He had no choice but to comply. He raised his hands and backed away, his heart pounding. The man stepped forward, his eyes narrowing as he examined the terminal.

"You've been busy," he said, a cruel smile playing on his lips. "But you're too late. The data is encrypted. You'll never crack it."

Alex glanced at his laptop, seeing the progress bar inching forward. He needed more time. "What do you want?"

The man shrugged. "To see you fail. To see your precious mission crumble to pieces."

Alex's mind worked frantically, searching for a way out. "And what about you? Do you think The Consortium will spare you if they succeed?"

The man's expression faltered for a moment, uncertainty flickering in his eyes. Alex seized the moment, lunging forward and knocking the gun from his hand. They grappled, each fighting for control. Alex's training kicked in, and he managed to disarm the man, sending him sprawling to the ground.

He grabbed his laptop and bolted for the door, his heart racing. "Thomas, I've got the data. I'm heading out."

"Roger that. We're ready for extraction. Get to the rendezvous point."

Alex ran through the corridors, the facility now on high alert. Alarms blared, and guards converged on his position. He ducked and weaved, using every ounce of his skill and agility to evade capture. He reached the perimeter and slipped through the maintenance gate, sprinting towards the extraction point.

A black SUV skidded to a halt, and the back door flew open. "Get in!" Thomas shouted.

Alex dove into the vehicle, and they sped away, the facility receding into the distance. He leaned back, gasping for breath, his heart still racing.

"You did it," Thomas said, a note of admiration in his voice. "We've got the evidence we need."

Alex nodded, his mind still reeling from the intensity of the mission. "What now?"

"Now we take down The Consortium for good."

As the city lights blurred past, Alex felt a renewed sense of determination. They had won a crucial battle, but the war was far from over. The final countdown had begun, and he was ready to see it through to the end.

8

Into the Lion's Den

The SUV sped through the city streets, leaving the industrial district and the now-compromised Consortium facility behind. The atmosphere inside the vehicle was electric with tension. Alex's mind raced, his body still coursing with adrenaline from the infiltration. Agent Thomas sat in the front seat, speaking urgently into his radio, coordinating the next steps with the team.

"Alex, you did great back there," Thomas said, turning to face him. "We've decrypted a portion of the data you retrieved. It contains plans for an imminent attack on several key infrastructures. We need to act fast."

Alex nodded, feeling the weight of the responsibility. "What do we do?"

"We've pinpointed a central command center for The Consortium," Thomas explained. "It's hidden in plain sight, within a high-rise building downtown. They're using it as their operational hub for coordinating these attacks. We need to shut it down before they can execute their plans."

The SUV screeched to a halt outside a nondescript office building, its glass facade reflecting the early morning light. The building seemed innocuous enough, but Alex knew better. He and Thomas exited the vehicle, joining a small team of agents already on site. They moved swiftly, entering the building and making their way to the elevator.

"The command center is on the top floor," Thomas said as the elevator doors closed. "We have to move quickly and quietly. They'll be expecting us after the facility breach."

The elevator ascended, the digital display counting up the floors. Alex's heart pounded in his chest. He glanced at Thomas, who gave him a reassuring nod. As the elevator neared the top floor, Thomas handed out earpieces and signaled for silence.

The doors opened with a soft chime, revealing a sleek, modern office space. The agents moved out, their weapons ready, scanning for any signs of trouble. The floor was eerily quiet, the only sound the soft hum of the air conditioning. They advanced down the hallway, past empty cubicles and conference rooms, until they reached a set of double doors marked "Authorized Personnel Only."

Thomas gestured for Alex to take point. He approached the doors, using his tools to bypass the electronic lock. The doors clicked open, revealing a large room filled with computer terminals, servers, and monitors displaying streams of data. At the center stood a group of people, busy at their stations, oblivious to the intruders.

"FBI! Hands where we can see them!" Thomas shouted, bursting into the room with the team.

Chaos erupted. The Consortium operatives scrambled, some reaching for weapons, others trying to shut down the systems. Alex ducked behind a console, returning fire as the agents engaged in a fierce firefight. Bullets whizzed past, striking equipment and shattering screens.

Alex spotted a man at the far end of the room, frantically typing at a terminal. He realized with a jolt that this must be the mastermind behind the planned attacks. Determined to stop him, Alex made his way through the chaos, using the cover of overturned desks and machinery.

As he closed in, the man turned, eyes widening in recognition. It was Victor Crane, his face twisted in a snarl. "You again," Crane spat, reaching for a hidden pistol. Alex lunged, knocking the gun from Crane's hand. They grappled, crashing into a row of servers, sending sparks flying.

"You're too late," Crane hissed, struggling against Alex's grip. "The attacks are already in motion."

Alex's mind raced. He glanced at the terminal, seeing a countdown timer ticking away. He knew he had to act fast. "Thomas, I need backup at the central terminal! Crane's trying to trigger the attacks!"

Thomas and another agent fought their way over, covering Alex as he worked to override the system. Crane laughed, a cruel, mocking sound. "You'll never stop it. The Consortium is everywhere."

Ignoring Crane's taunts, Alex focused on the terminal, his fingers flying over the keyboard. He accessed the encrypted files, searching for a way to halt the countdown. The timer continued its relentless march: 00:30... 00:29... 00:28...

"Come on, come on," Alex muttered, his heart pounding. He bypassed layer after layer of security, feeling the pressure mounting. Finally, he found the control sequence and entered the override code. The screen flashed, and the countdown froze at 00:05.

"It's done," Alex said, breathing a sigh of relief. "The attacks are stopped."

Crane's expression twisted with rage and defeat. "You think this is over?

There are others like me. You can't stop us all."

Thomas stepped forward, cuffing Crane and pulling him to his feet. "We'll see about that. For now, you're coming with us."

The room fell silent as the remaining operatives were subdued and secured. The team began gathering evidence, securing the data and equipment for further analysis. Alex leaned against a console, his body aching with exhaustion but his mind buzzing with the magnitude of what they had accomplished.

Thomas approached him, a look of respect in his eyes. "You did it, Alex. You stopped the attacks and took down their command center. This is a major blow to The Consortium."

Alex nodded, feeling a sense of grim satisfaction. "It's a start. But Crane's right. There are more out there. We have to keep fighting."

"We will," Thomas said. "But tonight, you need to get some rest. You've earned it."

As they made their way back to the SUV, the sun was fully risen, casting a golden light over the city. Alex thought of Emily and Lily, waiting for him at the safe house. He had faced the lion's den and emerged victorious, but he knew the battle was far from over. There were still shadows to uncover, threats to neutralize.

But for now, he allowed himself a moment of peace. The fight would continue, but so would his determination. He climbed into the SUV, ready for whatever lay ahead, knowing he had the strength and the will to see it through.

9

The Hidden Betrayal

The days following the raid on The Consortium's command center were a whirlwind of debriefings, data analysis, and strategic planning. Alex found little time to rest, his mind constantly racing with new information and emerging threats. He had become an integral part of the FBI's task force, his intimate knowledge of The Consortium proving invaluable. But the deeper they delved into the organization's inner workings, the more Alex felt an uneasy suspicion gnawing at him.

One evening, as the sun dipped below the horizon, Alex sat in the task force's makeshift headquarters, poring over a stack of decrypted documents. Emily and Lily were safe at the secure location, but his thoughts were never far from them. Agent Thomas approached, a grim expression on his face.

"Alex, we've found something troubling," Thomas said, sliding a file across the table. "It's a communication log between Crane and an unknown operative within our ranks. We have a mole."

Alex's blood ran cold. The idea of a traitor among them was a chilling prospect. He opened the file, scanning the messages. The details were vague, but the implications were clear: someone within the task force was feeding information to The Consortium.

"We need to identify this mole and neutralize them before they can do any more damage," Thomas continued. "But we have to be careful. If they suspect we're onto them, they could disappear or worse, sabotage our efforts."

Alex nodded, his mind racing. "Do we have any leads?"

Thomas shook his head. "Not yet. But we're monitoring all communications and movements closely. We need to proceed with caution."

Over the next few days, the tension within the task force grew palpable. Every glance, every conversation was tinged with suspicion. Alex found himself scrutinizing his colleagues, looking for any sign of betrayal. It was a delicate balancing act – maintaining the facade of normalcy while secretly hunting for the traitor.

Late one night, Alex was working alone in the dimly lit headquarters when his phone buzzed with a message. It was from an unknown number: "Meet me at the old warehouse on Pier 9. Come alone. I have information about the mole."

Alex's heart pounded. It could be a trap, but it could also be the break they needed. He grabbed his jacket and slipped out of the building, careful not to attract attention. The streets were quiet as he made his way to the waterfront, the cool night air heavy with anticipation.

The warehouse loomed ahead, a dark silhouette against the water. Alex approached cautiously, his senses on high alert. He slipped inside through a side door, the interior dimly lit by moonlight filtering through broken windows. He scanned the shadows, looking for any sign of movement.

A figure emerged from the darkness, their features obscured by a hood. "You came," the person said, their voice low and tense.

"Who are you?" Alex demanded, keeping his distance. "What do you know about the mole?"

The figure hesitated, then pulled back their hood, revealing a young woman with dark hair and piercing eyes. "My name is Sarah. I used to work for The Consortium, but I got out. I've been trying to take them down ever since."

Alex's skepticism was evident. "And why should I trust you?"

Sarah's eyes flashed with determination. "Because I know things you don't. The mole isn't just feeding them information. They're planning something big, something that could compromise everything you've worked for."

Alex's mind raced. "What are they planning?"

"An assassination," Sarah said, her voice trembling slightly. "They've targeted key members of the task force. If they succeed, it will cripple your efforts and give The Consortium the upper hand."

Alex felt a chill run down his spine. "Do you know who the mole is?"

Sarah nodded. "Yes. But I need your help to prove it. I have evidence, but it's hidden. I couldn't risk carrying it with me. It's at an old safe house outside the city. We need to go there now."

Alex weighed his options. It was risky, but if Sarah was telling the truth, they couldn't afford to waste any time. "Alright. Let's go."

They left the warehouse, driving through the city streets in tense silence. Sarah directed him to a remote area on the outskirts, where an abandoned house sat shrouded in darkness. They parked a distance away and approached on foot, the only sounds the crunch of gravel under their feet and the distant hum of the city.

Inside the safe house, Sarah led Alex to a hidden compartment beneath the floorboards. She retrieved a small metal box, opening it to reveal a flash drive and a stack of documents. "This is everything," she said, handing it to Alex. "Proof of the mole's identity and their plans."

Alex plugged the flash drive into his laptop, scanning the files. His eyes widened as he recognized the name: Special Agent Ryan, one of the task force's most trusted members. The documents detailed Ryan's communications with The Consortium, as well as plans for the upcoming assassination.

"We need to get this to Thomas," Alex said, his voice urgent. "Ryan can't know we're onto him."

Sarah nodded. "I'll stay here, out of sight. Go. Before it's too late."

Alex raced back to the headquarters, the weight of the evidence heavy in his hands. He found Thomas in the operations room, briefing the team. "Thomas, we have a problem," Alex said, pulling him aside. "I've identified the mole. It's Ryan."

Thomas's eyes widened in shock, but he quickly regained his composure. "Are you sure?"

"Positive," Alex said, showing him the evidence. "We need to act fast."

Thomas nodded, calling the team to attention. "We have a traitor in our midst. Special Agent Ryan has been working with The Consortium. We need to apprehend him immediately."

The task force sprang into action, surrounding Ryan's office. Ryan looked up in surprise as they entered, but his expression quickly turned to one of cold calculation. "What's this about?" he demanded.

"You know exactly what this is about," Thomas said, stepping forward. "We have proof of your betrayal. You're under arrest."

Ryan's eyes flicked to Alex, a sinister smile curling his lips. "You think this is over? You've only just begun to understand what you're up against."

As Ryan was led away, Alex felt a mix of relief and foreboding. They had uncovered the mole, but the battle against The Consortium was far from over. The hidden betrayal had been exposed, but the true fight was only just beginning.

10

The Trap

The arrest of Special Agent Ryan sent shockwaves through the task force. Trust had been shattered, and every member felt the weight of betrayal. Despite this, they couldn't afford to dwell on the past. With Ryan in custody, the team redoubled their efforts, focusing on the intelligence they had gathered and preparing for the imminent threat.

Alex, still reeling from the revelation of Ryan's duplicity, buried himself in the work. He spent hours analyzing data, mapping out The Consortium's network, and anticipating their next move. His thoughts frequently drifted to Emily and Lily, their safety a constant source of both comfort and concern. He knew he had to stay sharp; any lapse could cost them everything.

One evening, Alex received a coded message on his laptop. It was from an unknown source, but the encryption was familiar – it matched the patterns used by The Consortium. His heart raced as he decrypted the message: "The Consortium is planning a major operation tonight. Meet at the abandoned factory on 5th Street at midnight for details. Come alone."

Alex's first instinct was to inform Thomas, but a nagging suspicion held him back. If this was another trap, he couldn't risk compromising the entire team. Instead, he decided to go alone, but not without taking precautions. He prepared his gear, ensuring he had all the necessary tools and a concealed weapon. Before leaving, he left a note for Thomas detailing his whereabouts, just in case things went wrong.

The abandoned factory on 5th Street loomed ominously in the moonlight, its broken windows and crumbling walls a testament to years of neglect. Alex parked a distance away, his senses on high alert as he approached the entrance. The eerie silence was punctuated only by the sound of his footsteps on the gravel.

He slipped inside, his eyes adjusting to the darkness. The air was thick with dust, and the faint smell of rust and decay hung in the air. He moved cautiously, scanning the shadows for any sign of movement. Suddenly, a soft click echoed through the space, and a light flickered on.

A lone figure stood in the center of the room, their face obscured by the hood of a dark jacket. "Alex," the person said, their voice familiar yet distorted. "I'm glad you came."

"Who are you?" Alex demanded, his hand inching toward his concealed weapon. "What do you know about The Consortium's plans?"

The figure lowered their hood, revealing a man with sharp features and cold eyes. "My name is Harris. I used to be one of them, like Sarah. But I saw the light and decided to get out. I've been working against them from the inside."

Alex's grip tightened on his weapon. "Why should I trust you?"

Harris smiled, a cruel, calculating expression. "Because you have no choice. The Consortium is planning to take down the entire task force. Ryan's betrayal was just the beginning. They've planted bombs in your headquarters. If you don't act fast, everyone will be dead by morning."

Alex's blood ran cold. "How do I know you're telling the truth?"

Harris's smile faded, replaced by a look of grim determination. "You don't. But do you really want to take that risk?"

Before Alex could respond, a loud crash echoed through the factory. He turned to see several armed men entering the building, their guns trained on him and Harris. "Looks like they found us," Harris muttered, his hand reaching for a weapon of his own.

A firefight erupted, the sharp crack of gunfire reverberating through the factory. Alex ducked behind a stack of crates, returning fire as the armed men advanced. He caught a glimpse of Harris taking down one of the attackers, his movements swift and precise. Despite his initial mistrust, Alex found himself relying on Harris's skills as they fought side by side.

"Go! Get out of here!" Harris shouted, covering Alex as he made his way toward an exit. "You need to warn your team!"

Alex nodded, making a break for the door. He sprinted through the darkened factory, the sound of gunfire fading behind him. He burst into the night air, his heart pounding as he raced to his car. He had to get to the headquarters, had to stop the bombs before it was too late.

The drive felt like an eternity, every second a ticking clock in his mind. He pushed the car to its limits, weaving through the empty streets. As he neared the headquarters, he could see the lights still on, agents working late into the night. He screeched to a halt and ran inside, shouting for Thomas.

"Bombs! The Consortium planted bombs!" Alex yelled, his voice echoing through the corridors.

Thomas appeared, his face a mask of concern. "Where? How do you know?"

"No time to explain," Alex said, pulling out his phone and showing Thomas the message. "We need to evacuate and find those bombs."

The task force sprang into action, the building a flurry of movement as agents searched for the explosives. Alex joined the search, his mind racing. Minutes ticked by, each one feeling like an eternity. Then, he heard a shout from one of the agents.

"Found one! In the basement!"

Alex and Thomas rushed to the basement, where a small, sleek device was attached to the wall. The timer was counting down – five minutes left. Alex's hands shook as he examined the bomb, his training kicking in. He worked quickly, carefully cutting wires and disabling the mechanism.

"Done," he said, breathing a sigh of relief. "But there could be more."

They continued their search, finding and disabling two more bombs. Finally, the building was declared safe, and the exhausted team gathered in the operations room.

Thomas looked at Alex, his expression one of gratitude and respect. "You saved us tonight. But we still have a long fight ahead."

Alex nodded, feeling the weight of their situation. The trap had been set, but they had survived. Now, more determined than ever, he knew they had to take the fight to The Consortium and end the threat once and for all.

11

The Double Cross

The task force's narrow escape from the bomb plot had left everyone on edge. Alex, exhausted but resolute, knew that they were running out of time. The Consortium's plans were escalating, and every minute counted. With Ryan in custody, they had a key piece of the puzzle, but they needed to act swiftly to stay ahead of the organization's next move.

The next morning, Thomas called an emergency meeting. The room buzzed with tension as agents took their seats, their faces reflecting the strain of the last few days. Thomas stood at the head of the table, his expression grave.

"We've analyzed the data from Ryan's files," Thomas began. "There's a high-level meeting between The Consortium's leaders happening tonight. It's our chance to take down their command structure in one strike."

A map of the city appeared on the screen behind Thomas, highlighting a secluded mansion on the outskirts. "This is where they'll be. It's heavily guarded, but we have a plan to infiltrate and apprehend the key figures."

Alex leaned forward, studying the layout. "What's the plan?"

Thomas outlined a detailed strategy, dividing the team into specialized units. Alex was assigned to the infiltration team, tasked with entering the mansion and securing the leaders. It was a high-risk operation, but the potential payoff was immense. If they could capture the top brass, it would cripple The Consortium's operations.

As dusk fell, the team gathered in the staging area, checking their equipment and reviewing the plan one last time. Alex felt a knot of anticipation in his stomach. This was it – the culmination of their efforts. He thought of Emily and Lily, drawing strength from the thought of keeping them safe.

The convoy of unmarked vehicles moved out, navigating the winding roads to the mansion. The moon was hidden behind thick clouds, casting the landscape in shadows. Alex rode in silence, his mind focused on the task ahead. They parked a distance away, approaching on foot to avoid detection.

The mansion loomed before them, its grandeur masked by the darkness. The team split into their assigned units, moving into position. Alex's group approached the rear entrance, using the cover of trees and shrubs. He felt his pulse quicken as they reached the door, his senses on high alert.

Using his tools, Alex bypassed the security system, and they slipped inside. The interior was opulent, a stark contrast to the tension-filled atmosphere. They moved silently through the halls, communicating through hand signals and earpieces. Every shadow seemed to hold a potential threat.

As they neared the central meeting room, Alex's heart pounded. He peered around a corner, spotting two guards outside the door. He signaled to his team, and they moved swiftly, taking down the guards with precision. Alex pressed his ear to the door, hearing muffled voices inside.

Thomas's voice crackled in his earpiece. "Infiltration team, prepare to breach on my signal."

Alex nodded to his team, and they took their positions. The seconds stretched out, the anticipation almost unbearable. Then, the signal came.

"Go!"

They burst through the door, weapons drawn, shouting commands. The room erupted into chaos. High-ranking members of The Consortium scrambled, some reaching for weapons, others trying to flee. Alex's team moved with practiced efficiency, subduing the leaders and securing the room.

Alex's eyes scanned the room, his gaze landing on a man at the head of the table. It was Victor Crane. Their eyes locked, and Crane's expression twisted into a smirk.

"Alex," Crane said, his voice dripping with contempt. "You've been a thorn in our side for too long."

"You're done, Crane," Alex replied, his voice steady despite the adrenaline coursing through him. "This ends now."

Crane laughed, a cold, mirthless sound. "You think capturing us will stop The Consortium? We're just one part of a much larger machine."

As Crane spoke, Alex noticed something off about the situation. The leaders seemed too calm, too prepared. His eyes flicked to a briefcase on the table. He moved quickly, opening it to reveal a laptop and several devices. The screen displayed a countdown.

"It's a trap!" Alex shouted, realizing the truth. "They've set us up!"

The countdown ticked down: 00:10... 00:09... 00:08...

Panic surged through the room. "Everyone out! Now!" Thomas's voice boomed through the earpiece.

Alex and his team scrambled, dragging the captured leaders with them. They raced through the halls, the countdown echoing in their ears. They burst through the rear entrance, sprinting for cover. Just as they reached the treeline, an explosion ripped through the mansion, a massive fireball lighting up the night sky.

The shockwave knocked Alex off his feet, and he hit the ground hard. He lay there for a moment, dazed, before struggling to his feet. The mansion was engulfed in flames, the air thick with smoke and debris. He saw his team regrouping, ensuring everyone was accounted for.

Thomas approached, his face grim. "Is everyone alright?"

Alex nodded, his mind racing. "We've got Crane and a few others. But they knew we were coming. This was planned."

Thomas's expression hardened. "We'll get answers from them. For now, we need to regroup and assess the damage."

As they moved to a safe distance, Alex couldn't shake the feeling of unease. The trap had been set, and they had walked right into it. The Consortium was always one step ahead, their reach extending further than he had imagined.

Back at the headquarters, the task force interrogated the captured leaders, extracting whatever information they could. Crane remained defiant, his eyes gleaming with a sinister confidence.

"You think this is a victory?" Crane sneered. "You're playing a game you can't win."

Alex stared at him, a mix of determination and anger burning in his eyes.

"We'll see about that."

As the night wore on, the task force worked tirelessly, piecing together the fragments of their shattered plan. Alex knew the battle was far from over. The Consortium was a hydra – cutting off one head only revealed more. But he also knew that they had struck a significant blow, capturing key figures and disrupting their operations.

In the quiet moments before dawn, Alex allowed himself a brief respite. He thought of Emily and Lily, drawing strength from the love and determination that drove him. The path ahead was fraught with danger, but he was resolved to see it through.

As the first light of morning broke over the horizon, Alex stood with Thomas, watching the sun rise. They had survived the trap, but the true fight was only just beginning. The Consortium was a formidable enemy, but Alex's determination burned brighter than ever. He would stop at nothing to protect his family and bring the organization to its knees.

And so, with the dawn of a new day, the battle continued.

12

The Final Gambit

In the aftermath of the failed raid and subsequent explosion, the task force found themselves back at headquarters, battered but not broken. The captured leaders of The Consortium had provided little useful information under interrogation, their resolve unyielding. Victor Crane's sinister confidence remained unshaken, his eyes always glinting with the knowledge of something dark and foreboding.

As Alex walked through the hallways, the weight of recent events pressed heavily upon him. The stakes had never been higher. Emily and Lily's faces filled his thoughts, fueling his determination. He knew that the next move could mean the difference between victory and devastating loss.

Thomas approached Alex, a folder in his hand and a grim expression on his face. "We've received new intelligence," he said, his voice low. "It's from an anonymous source, but it matches the patterns we've seen before. They're planning something big, and soon."

Alex took the folder, flipping it open. Inside were detailed schematics of a high-profile event: a diplomatic summit scheduled to take place in two days, attended by international leaders and dignitaries. The threat was clear — The Consortium intended to strike, sending a message that no one was beyond their reach.

"This is their final gambit," Alex muttered, studying the plans. "We need to be ready for anything."

Thomas nodded. "We've already started preparations. We'll have teams in place, security tightened, and every angle covered. But Alex, this is personal for you. I need you to be sharp, to stay focused."

Alex met Thomas's gaze, the resolve in his eyes unwavering. "I won't let them win. Not this time."

The next forty-eight hours were a blur of activity. The task force coordinated with international security agencies, meticulously planning every detail. Alex and his team conducted surveillance, analyzed potential threats, and devised contingency plans. The atmosphere was electric with tension, every agent acutely aware of the gravity of the situation.

On the morning of the summit, the city buzzed with anticipation. Streets were cordoned off, and security checkpoints were established at every entrance. Alex, dressed in tactical gear, stood with his team, their faces set with determination. The stakes were clear — this was their chance to stop The Consortium once and for all.

As the summit began, Alex monitored the proceedings from a control room filled with screens and communication equipment. He watched as dignitaries arrived, their entourages closely scrutinized by security personnel. Everything seemed to be running smoothly, but a sense of unease lingered in the air.

Suddenly, a commotion on one of the screens caught Alex's attention. A delivery van had breached one of the checkpoints, speeding toward the venue.

Security forces moved to intercept, but the van swerved, crashing through a barricade. The back doors flew open, and armed men poured out, their intentions unmistakable.

"Code red! We have a breach!" Alex shouted into his earpiece, springing into action.

Chaos erupted as the gunmen opened fire, targeting the venue. Security forces engaged, and a fierce firefight broke out. Alex and his team rushed to the scene, weaving through the panicked crowd. The air was filled with the sounds of gunfire, shouts, and the screams of civilians caught in the crossfire.

Alex's training took over, his movements precise and calculated. He spotted a group of gunmen advancing toward the main hall, where the dignitaries were gathered. He signaled to his team, and they moved to intercept. The firefight was intense, bullets whizzing past as they exchanged fire with the attackers.

One by one, they took down the gunmen, clearing a path to the main hall. As they approached, Alex noticed a familiar figure among the attackers. Victor Crane stood at the entrance, a cold smile on his face as he directed his men.

"Crane!" Alex shouted, his voice cutting through the din.

Crane turned, his smile widening. "Alex. I was hoping you'd make it. Here for the grand finale, are we?"

"This ends now," Alex said, his grip tightening on his weapon.

Crane's eyes gleamed with malice. "You're too late. The bombs are already in place. In a few minutes, this building will be rubble."

Alex's heart raced. He scanned the room, his mind racing. They needed to find the bombs and disarm them, and fast. He signaled to his team, and they fanned out, searching for any signs of explosives.

As Alex moved through the hall, his eyes caught a glint of metal beneath a table. He crouched down, carefully inspecting the device. It was a sophisticated bomb, the timer ticking down with ominous finality. He reached for his tools, his hands steady despite the urgency.

"Alex, we've found another one!" came a voice over his earpiece. "North wing, under the stage."

Alex's mind raced. There were likely more bombs, strategically placed to ensure maximum destruction. They had to work quickly, methodically. He focused on the bomb in front of him, carefully cutting wires and disabling the trigger mechanism. The timer stopped, and he breathed a sigh of relief.

"Bomb disarmed," he reported. "Moving to the next one."

He sprinted to the north wing, where his teammate was already working on the bomb under the stage. Together, they disarmed it, their movements synchronized and efficient. As they moved to the next location, Alex's earpiece crackled with updates – bombs found and disarmed, but still more to go.

In the main hall, Crane watched the chaos unfold, his smile never wavering. He moved with the confidence of someone who believed he had already won. Alex spotted him, a surge of anger and determination propelling him forward.

He confronted Crane, their eyes locking. "It's over, Crane. Your plan has failed."

Crane laughed, a hollow, chilling sound. "You're a fool, Alex. Do you really think you can stop all of them?"

Alex's jaw tightened. "Watch me."

With a final, defiant glance, Crane made a break for the exit. Alex pursued, his focus unyielding. They raced through the hallways, the sounds of the ongoing battle fading into the background. As they reached the exit, Crane turned, a gun in his hand.

Alex dove for cover as shots rang out, the bullets thudding into the walls around him. He returned fire, his movements swift and precise. The exchange was brief but intense, and finally, Crane fell, a look of shock and disbelief on his face.

Alex approached, his weapon trained on Crane. "It's over," he said, his voice steady. "You've lost."

Crane's eyes darkened, his breath labored. "You think you've won? This is just the beginning. There are others, more powerful than you can imagine."

Alex stared down at him, the weight of the moment pressing in. "We'll find them. And we'll stop them."

As Crane's eyes closed for the last time, Alex felt a mix of relief and determination. They had averted disaster, but the fight was far from over. He rejoined his team, who had successfully disarmed the remaining bombs. The threat had been neutralized, but the war against The Consortium would continue.

With the immediate danger behind them, Alex allowed himself a moment to breathe. He thought of Emily and Lily, their faces a beacon of hope and strength. He knew that as long as he had them, he would continue to fight, no matter the cost.

As the sun set on the city, the task force regrouped, their resolve stronger than ever. The final gambit had been played, but the battle for justice and safety continued. And Alex, with his unwavering determination, stood ready to face whatever came next.